LOUIS PASTEUR

THE GERM KILLER

Herschel Levit

LOUIS PASTEUR

THE GERM KILLER

By John Mann

Illustrated by Herschel Levit

The Macmillan Company, New York
Collier-Macmillan Limited, London

Library of Congress catalog card number: 65-15577
The Macmillan Company, New York
Collier-Macmillan Canada, Ltd., Toronto, Ontario
Printed in the United States of America

First Printing

LOUIS PASTEUR

THE GERM KILLER

On a quiet day in 1822, Louis Pasteur was born. His family, who lived in the little French village of Dôle, were loving, hard-working, and patriotic. His mother, Jeanne, was a simple countrywoman. His father, Jean, once a soldier with the Emperor Napoleon I, now made his living as a tanner, drying the skins of animals and selling them to people who made jackets, coats, and caps from them.

When Louis was still a boy, his family moved to the nearby town of Arbois, where his father thought that he could make a better living. On long summer days Louis liked to watch his father work as he carefully cleaned animal skins and stretched them to dry. He also liked to catch fish with the other boys of the town.

One thing Louis did not like was joining the other boys in trapping birds. It seemed to him that birds should be left free to roam the skies. No one who saw him then thought that one day Louis Pasteur would be a great man. Like many other children his age, he seemed only a thoughtful, quiet boy.

1

Nevertheless, his parents, like most parents, hoped that Louis would be more successful than they had been. And when at the age of thirteen Louis became interested in art, his family thought he might become a painter.

"It is a good kind of work," his mother said, "even if it will not make him a fortune."

"The money makes little difference—if painting is what he wants to do," his father said firmly.

For a time it did seem that this was what Louis wanted. He painted many pictures, using friends and family as his subjects. He had ability, and the pictures were good.

Fortunately for us and for the world, Louis Pasteur changed his mind. He did not become an artist. Instead, he decided to become a science teacher. One of his own instructors, a Monsieur Romanet, encouraged him, for he saw that beneath Louis's apparent calmness there was something unusual that no one else, not even Louis himself, seemed to understand.

When Louis was fifteen, Monsieur Romanet had a serious talk with the boy's parents. "Your Louis," he said, "has a special talent, but it has not been noticed."

Louis's mother put her arms around her son proudly. She had never doubted that her son was exceptional.

"You see," continued the teacher, "he works very carefully. Most people think he is not very smart. But they are wrong. He just wants to be sure that he is right before he says anything. I think Louis will go far, but only if he gets the proper education. You must send him to Paris to prepare for the university."

"Now, just one minute," said Jean Pasteur after Monsieur Romanet left. "Paris is a long way off. Louis has never been away before. I think he is too young for such a trip."

"And who will wash and cook for him?" said Jeanne.

So they talked on into the night. Louis himself said

almost nothing. He was proud and frightened at the same time. In the end, the decision was made for him. He would go to Paris.

Louis left for the capital of France on a day that was cool and misty. His whole family gathered to see him off. His father helped him up to the seat next to the driver of the coach and told him, "Be good, my boy. Study hard, and if you ever need us, we will be there."

The driver was in a hurry. There was hardly time to wave good-by before the coach disappeared in the mist that rested on the low mountains surrounding the town. Louis Pasteur was off on his first big adventure.

From the beginning, Louis was unhappy. The Paris streets were narrow, the houses high, the people strange, and the air was not the clean, cool air of Arbois. Although Monsieur Barbet, the man with whom he stayed, tried to be kind, Louis was homesick and unhappy. He could not do his schoolwork. He could not eat. He began to have strange dreams. Monsieur Barbet saw what was happening and worried. Finally, he decided he must write to Jean Pasteur.

A few days later, Louis was told that someone was waiting for him in a nearby restaurant. At first he did not want to go. Then he thought, "Maybe it's someone from home." He ran out the door. When he got to the restaurant he saw that it was not a neighbor, but his father!

"I have come to take you home, Louis," his father said. Louis thought of the familiar streets and the people he had known all his life. He was too happy to say anything.

When Louis returned home to Arbois he decided he must have more time to prepare himself for the examinations he must take to enter the great university in Paris. He needed more time to prepare for Paris itself.

He was right. It was only after several years of hard work that he passed the examinations. Then he began

Herschel Levit

his work at the university. He felt very different now—about himself and what he wanted to do.

From the start, Pasteur was interested in crystals and their beautiful shapes. He was fascinated by the way they shine like jewels when light goes through them. He tried to understand why they can take on different forms and how their shapes affect their reactions to light, heat, and different chemicals. For a time it looked as if Louis Pasteur would spend his life studying these shining crystals.

But one day when Pasteur was busy in his laboratory, bent over his microscope, a Monsieur Bigo came in.

"Have you brought me some new crystals?" Pasteur asked, looking up from his microscope.

"Oh no," laughed Monsieur Bigo, "nothing like that. I am a wine maker."

"But what has that to do with me?" Louis said, a little puzzled.

"Lately I have been having trouble," said Monsieur Bigo. "My wines have been turning sour, and I don't know what is wrong. Can you help me?"

"I am very busy," said Pasteur. The wine maker looked dejected. "And besides, there is no guarantee that I can help you," Louis added.

Monsieur Bigo could not see that Louis was really

busy because nothing seemed to be happening in the laboratory. There were only Pasteur and his equipment. But he didn't want the scientist to become angry, so he said, "It would be a great favor to me if you would come to my wine factory."

"All right," Pasteur said finally, "I will come to your winery and see what I can find."

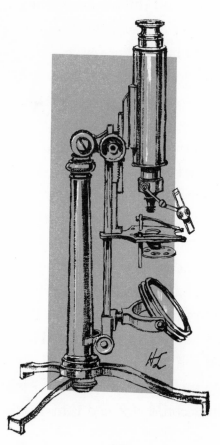

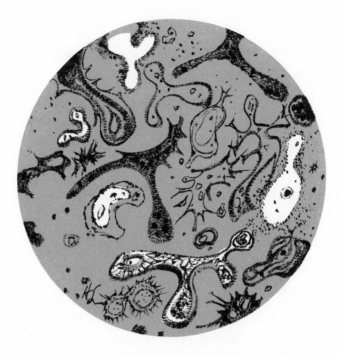

A few weeks later Pasteur appeared at Monsieur Bigo's wine-making factory. He took with him only a microscope and a small stove, but these were enough. He looked at different kinds of wine under his microscope: white wines, red wines, sour wines, sweet wines, spoiled wines, and perfect wines. And as he looked he saw something that made him excited. There were tiny animals in the wine! At first, he wasn't even sure whether they were plants or animals. It was hard to tell because they did not look like anything he had ever seen before. They were just little bodies you could

11

see only if you used a microscope. They moved around in the wine. Some seemed to propel themselves, while others moved only by the action of the wine when it was stirred or shaken.

One fact was certain, however—they were all alive, and they could grow. Even more startling, they divided themselves so that one animal became two! Pasteur had stepped into a new world; later his self-dividing creatures would be called "germs" or "microbes."

This universe of small creatures was not a simple world. Louis Pasteur soon discovered that there were many kinds of things that could go wrong with wines because of these germs. The wines could taste too flat or too sharp, too bitter or too sweet. And each time a wine tasted bad there was a different reason to explain it. He continued to study. He went to the big barrels where the wine was stored, and talked to the workmen about their problems. He examined all the wines under his microscope. All this work slowly led him to one conclusion: The "little animals" (germs) were responsible for spoiling the wine.

"Monsieur Bigo," he said one day, "it all comes down to this. The germs grow and the wine gets too sweet or sour or flat or bitter. If we kill these animals the wine will be better."

"But," said Monsieur Bigo, "how can this be? These animals are so very small we cannot even see them without that microscope you use. How can they cause all this harm?"

"Who knows how much harm they can cause? Perhaps they could even make people sick if they grew inside them," said Pasteur. "I have been experimenting

with various ways of killing them. I have been thinking of freezing them or passing electricity through them. But I have discovered that the best and simplest way is heat. If you heat the wine for several minutes the germs will be killed and the wine will stay fresh."

"We will try," said Monsieur Bigo excitedly. "And

if you are right, we will name the method after you." The process did work, and it was called "pasteurization"—"Pasteur's treatment."

Best of all, Pasteur's method worked not only for wine but also for other liquids, such as beer and milk. Today all the milk that we drink is "pasteurized." Monsieur Bigo was delighted, but Pasteur was not interested in wine making alone. It was the "little animals" that fascinated him. Pasteur began to look for them everywhere: in water, in food, in the air. And everywhere he looked, he found them. They had different shapes and sizes, but there they were, wherever he looked. He had only to put a little piece of food or water under his microscope and he could see them—eating, growing, dividing.

Pasteur began to suspect that these tiny creatures must ride the winds to be spread to every corner of the earth. He suspected, too, that they must be carried by the dust in the air. To prove this, he decided to show that if there were no dust there would be no microbes, or germs.

Louis made himself special little bottles with long, curved necks. In the bottles he put a little liquid that would be spoiled by germs if they reached it and started to grow.

"You see," said Pasteur one day to another scientist, "the dust will not reach the liquid. It will rest in the long, curved necks of the bottles. If the little animals are riding on the dust, the liquid should not spoil."

Pasteur waited patiently for many days to see what would happen. The liquid stayed clear. No germs had reached it. Pasteur was pleased, but the experiment could not stop here; he must let different kinds of dust reach the liquid to see what would happen. To do this, he boiled the liquid until all the air was out of the bottle. Then he sealed the end of the bottle. He went into cellars, into buildings and down many streets. In each place he would break open the neck of a carefully prepared bottle and expose the liquid to the dust-filled air. If the dust in the air carried the "little animals," the

liquid would be spoiled. If there were no microbes in the dust, the liquid would remain as it had been. People watched the strange scientist, opening bottles and closing them again in every nook and cranny he could find. Pasteur didn't mind what people said. He even opened a few bottles near his home, Arbois. His old friends shrugged their shoulders and said, "Oh well, he is famous now. Who can say what a famous man will do?"

Pasteur finally decided that the best way to prove his idea was to climb a mountain and open some bottles high up where there was little or no dust. He hired a guide and a mule and climbed to the top of the highest mountain he could find. There, he opened twenty of his specially prepared bottles. The liquid in only one of the twenty bottles became spoiled. Pasteur had proved he was right. The microbes *were* carried by the dust in the air. Where there was almost no dust there was almost none of the tiny animals to spoil the liquid.

Some people listened to Pasteur when he talked

Herschel Levit

about what he had found, but just as many did not. The men who didn't believe Pasteur were very outspoken about their feelings. "You are always talking about these little animals. They are not important. They may be interesting to watch, but what do they have to do with us?"

Pasteur, however, paid no attention. He knew what he believed and what he had found. "Germs *are* everywhere," he said, "and some of them are dangerous."

Now he began going to hospitals to watch doctors operate. He was unhappy to see that no effort was made to kill the germs in or near open wounds. Pasteur spoke to the doctors.

"If you don't keep the germs away, they will make your patients sick. They will get into the cuts and grow. You *must* kill them. You *must* keep them from reaching the cuts."

But the doctors did not believe him. After all, who was he? He wasn't even a doctor. They went on operating as they had always done. Many of their patients died because of infections caused by the microbes Pasteur had warned them about, but the doctors refused to believe that germs had anything to do with these deaths.

It made Pasteur miserable to see all these people

die, miserable and angry. Why would no one listen to him?

But someone had. In England, a surgeon named Joseph Lister carefully studied Pasteur's work and decided that he was right. For ten years Lister worked to develop a way of keeping germs out of open wounds. The results were astonishing. Wounds no longer became infected. Fewer and fewer of his patients died after their operations. Lister wrote to Pasteur, giving him credit for his success: "What I have done," said Lister, "was based on your work."

Now Pasteur felt very proud. His studies of germs had opened the door to modern surgery!

Pasteur was now becoming more famous all the time, and when he spoke, other scientists listened. Dozens of people began coming to him with strange

requests. There was a disease affecting silkworms. Would Pasteur study it? Pigs were getting sick. Could Monsieur Pasteur look at them? Usually, Pasteur said yes. He went to the farms and the villages where the particular disease was found. He hunted for the germ responsible for the sickness and looked for a way to kill it or keep it from growing.

By now, Pasteur had several assistants to help him. They were studying a disease called chicken cholera. The disease was killing off thousands of the chickens that many farmers depended on to help make their living.

Pasteur found the germ that caused this cholera. When it was injected into healthy chickens, they soon became sick.

During these experiments, something unexpected happened, and Pasteur and his assistants were interrupted by a more urgent matter. It was two or three weeks before they returned to the problem of chicken cholera. When they did, they took the weeks-old germs and injected them into healthy chickens as they had been doing before their studies were interrupted.

The next day Pasteur came to his laboratory. The chickens were still alive! An astonished assistant stared into the cages. "The disease should have killed them!"

"Perhaps there is a relationship between the age of a germ and its strength," Pasteur thoughtfully told his assistants. "The old germs that we used may have been weakened. Now we must try the experiment again—using new microbes."

The scientist began the new test. But there weren't enough new chickens. He took the old ones that had not died from the first inoculation and gave them the new strong germs as well. "This time," he thought, "they will surely die."

The next morning when Pasteur got to the laboratory, he was tired. It was very early. He always arrived much earlier than anyone else. What he saw disappointed him. He thought the tests had failed. Some of

the chickens were still alive. "The injections weren't strong enough," he muttered.

But then Pasteur took a second look, and for a moment he couldn't believe his eyes. All the *new* chickens were dead. It was only the chickens that had received the first injection that were still alive.

An hour later, when his assistants came into the laboratory, they found Pasteur talking to himself and frantically making notes. He seemed very excited.

"What is it?" they cried, thinking that Pasteur was suffering from overwork.

"We've found it, we've found it! It was an accident but we *have* found it."

"Found what?" they asked rather doubtfully.

"We've found the secret of turning these 'little animals' against themselves. We've discovered a way that they can fight themselves instead of killing the chickens." Pasteur looked off into space. "There's no telling how far or where this may lead."

The assistants looked at the dead chickens and at the live ones. Slowly they realized that the ones which had received the old weak germs first were still alive. The ones which had not had that first injection were dead. The old and weak germs had protected the chickens against the stronger germs they had been given later, only the day before.

"If this will work for one disease," said Pasteur, "it should work for others. It will only be necessary to find a way in each case of weakening these small creatures so that they can protect an animal or a human being against a disease without causing a strong attack of the disease itself."

Pasteur quickly decided to see if he was right. He had been studying a disease called anthrax which attacks sheep. It is a serious illness that killed as many as one out of ten in a sheepfold.

Although he already knew a great deal about anthrax, Pasteur did not know how to prevent it. Now he

24

thought he might have the answer. Only it was not as easy as he expected. If he stored the anthrax germs in the laboratory a few weeks, they didn't get weaker. They simply changed their form and remained as strong as ever. He worked desperately and far into the night

to find out how to weaken the germs. Finally, he thought he had it.

If he kept the germs in the right fluid at the right temperature for the right length of time, the germs were weakened. "The weak germs," Pasteur said hopefully, "will protect the sheep from the strong ones."

Pasteur tried out the weak germs in the laboratory.

25

The sheep seemed to be protected, but the sheep farmers were not convinced. They wanted proof—and on a farm, not in a laboratory. A great experiment was set up, to be conducted on a nearby farm. Pasteur would inject twenty-five sheep with weak germs. Then these twenty-five and another twenty-five unprotected sheep would receive a large amount of fresh, and therefore strong, anthrax germs. "The sheep that have been given weak germs first will live," Pasteur said. "The others will die."

On a sunny day in May, Pasteur and his assistants went to the farm and began to give the sheep the weakened germs which they hoped would protect them. From all over the country animal doctors and scientists came to watch. Many hoped to see Pasteur prove that he had a cure for anthrax. Many others wanted to see Pasteur fail. "He's too sure of himself," these doctors said.

It took many days for Pasteur to give the weak germs to the twenty-five sheep in just the way that he thought would be most effective. But finally the day came to give all the sheep the strong germs. Pasteur worked with his assistants, carefully giving each sheep the proper dosage of the new germs. Many people said openly that in two days all the sheep would be dead. Pasteur himself said nothing. He was confident in his own work. He could not fail. He must not!

The next day was an anxious one for Pasteur. One of his assistants visited the farm and told him that, as expected, the unprotected sheep were getting weak, but one of the protected sheep as well seemed to have

a fever. Suddenly, Louis felt that he *might* fail. Perhaps a mistake had been made: the first injection of germs had been too weak; someone had made an error; anything could have happened.

Pasteur did not sleep that night, but the morning brought good news. The sheep he had protected were all alive! The others were dead or dying.

Pasteur rode back to the farm. Great crowds of people were waiting for him. As he arrived in his carriage, a few people began to clap. Slowly, more and more people joined in until all of them were clapping and cheering. Pasteur was now a hero. He had saved the sheep, and his friends were convinced that this was only the beginning.

Even though he was getting old (he was now sixty), he did not stop working. He couldn't; for Louis, his work had always been his life. He slowed down a little, but only a little. Now he turned his attention to a new disease, a strange disease called rabies. It affects dogs and, through them, human beings. When a dog has rabies he is called "rabid," or mad. In this condition he foams at the mouth and often bites people. When a person is bitten by a mad dog, he may get rabies himself, but not until four weeks later. It is a long, painful disease. Before Pasteur's work on it, the person who

was bitten by one of these "mad dogs" usually died.

No one knew the cause of rabies or its cure. Pasteur decided that he would find out. Very shortly he discovered that he had taken on the hardest job of his life.

To begin with, Pasteur could not find the microbe that was responsible. "It must be there," Pasteur muttered, bending down and peering into his microscope. "If only I can find it." Finally he decided that the germ was too small to see even with a microscope.

One day as Pasteur sat in his laboratory looking at the rabid dogs in their cages around him, he thought, "There is one thing about rabies that is very strange. It takes so long to get it after a person is bitten—almost a month. If only there were some way to prevent the disease from growing immediately after the person is bitten, then we would have a real cure."

Suddenly, the howling of one of the mad dogs interrupted his thoughts. He watched as the dog jumped at him, stopped only by the bars of its cage. This was dangerous work that Pasteur was doing. The mad dogs themselves were highly dangerous; even their spit was threatening, since it carried the invisible rabies germs. Louis and his assistants had to be very careful.

As time passed, Pasteur found a way to weaken rabies germs. When he injected these germs into healthy dogs they did not get sick. Finally he put the inoculated dogs into cages with the rabid animals. The healthy dogs were bitten savagely. But as time passed Pasteur kept on with his treatment of the normal animals. They did not get sick.

It seemed that Pasteur had found a way to prevent rabies in dogs by giving them repeated doses of the

weak germs. Perhaps he had beaten rabies as well as anthrax!

Then one day a little boy was brought into Pasteur's laboratory by his mother.

"How do you do?" Pasteur rose from his laboratory stool. "What can I do for you?"

"We have come to you for help," said the woman desperately. "My little boy, Joseph, has been badly bitten by a mad dog. Our doctor thought that you could help us. He says that there is nothing he can do."

Pasteur looked at the little boy; the child was in pain and could hardly walk. But Pasteur had never tried his treatment on human beings. He had no idea if it would work. It might hurt the boy instead of saving him. If the boy died, people would call Pasteur a criminal.

32

What should he do? It was the most difficult decision of his life.

Pasteur said, "Come back this afternoon. I must think about it."

Pasteur then went out to talk to some doctors about the child. They all told him, "Go ahead. The case is so serious that there is nothing to lose."

Later in the afternoon, when Joseph and his mother returned, Pasteur began the treatment. Before Pasteur gave Joseph the weakened germs, Joseph had been sobbing uncontrollably. Afterward he grew calm. His mother put him to bed and he slept easily. But Pasteur got very little rest. Anxiously, he waited for morning. When he saw that Joseph was still all right, he regained a little of his confidence.

The treatments continued for the next ten days. They were, for Pasteur, the longest ten days of his life. In the middle of the night, he would awake with a start, expecting the worst news of all—that the child had died. When he did sleep, he had dreams of Joseph's getting sick. His fears were groundless. Each morning Joseph seemed to be getting better.

At the end of the ten days there was nothing further that Pasteur could do. Louis was exhausted, physically and mentally. Still unsure of his success, he went to the

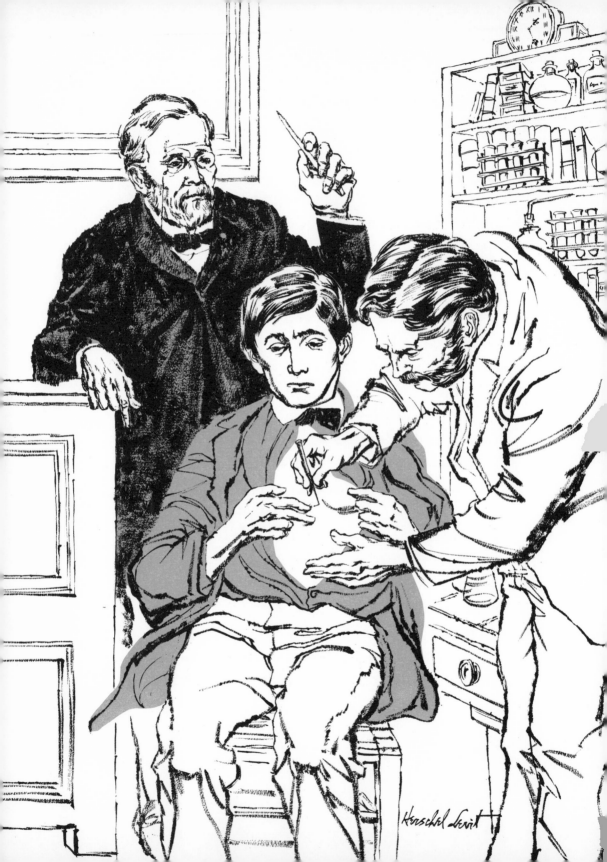

Herschel Levit

country to rest. He still dreaded a telegram telling him that something had gone wrong.

The telegram never came. A month went by. The boy had recovered.

Pasteur had indeed found a cure for rabies!

Word of his success spread like wildfire. From all over the country, from all over the world, people who had been bitten by rabid dogs rushed to Pasteur for his new treatment.

Pasteur worked and worked to make the weakened germs and give them to all the people who came to him for help. He watched how everything was done, and talked to all his patients.

He liked the children especially. He always had a piece of candy or a coin in his pocket to give them, and they in turn felt that he was like their grandfather, kind and wise. They never realized how weary the scientist was.

Pasteur had driven himself all his life. Now, though he did not know it, his working days were drawing to a close. More and more often he had to rest. Reluctantly, he agreed to go to the south of France to gain back some of his strength in the warm sunshine.

While he was away, money was gathered from all over France to erect a great building to carry on the work that he had started. Many other nations contributed as well. It was to be called the Pasteur Institute.

When Louis returned to Paris, he liked to watch the workmen as they brought the building to life. His Institute would be a place where people would study the small animals, the germs and microbes, that he had discovered.

His Institute was his final achievement, which would remain after he was gone. Pasteur felt very content watching it grow until it was finished.

As the years passed, Pasteur took what part he could in the work of the day. He had his office in the Insti-

tute. He checked the work in progress and visited with important people who came to see him.

On Pasteur's seventieth birthday a great party was held in the famous hall of the Sorbonne University. Members of the government were present. The heads of all the scientific groups in France were there. A great audience filled the hall. At 10:30 in the morning trumpets sounded. Pasteur entered with the President of France. He went slowly to the seat of honor. He listened as the great men of the day praised him and his work.

But Louis could not rest on this admiration while he had any strength left. Although he could no longer work himself, he remained interested in the work of others. Eagerly he examined the new germs they uncovered and was as delighted as though these were his own discoveries.

"Yes," he would say, "there are my little animals. I have spent most of my life looking at them, studying them, learning how to tame them. They are like big animals, you know. Some of the small ones are like tiny lions and tigers—dangerous. Others are dogs and cats—friendly. We must learn to live with them all. You must go on studying them, learning to know their habits. I have opened the way for you. Now you, my students, must go on and see where the road will lead."

For Pasteur himself the road had ended. At the age of seventy-four, he died peacefully. He was given a great funeral at the mighty Cathedral of Notre Dame. People lined the street as far as the eye could see. He was buried in the Pasteur Institute, as he would have wished.

His work went on. Really, it had just begun. In less than fifteen years, sixty Pasteur Institutes had sprung up around the world. In all of them, scientists studied the "little animals" to which Louis Pasteur had devoted his life.

Today Louis Pasteur is still very much alive. Wherever people study germs, and try to find ways to weaken them to save human lives, Louis Pasteur's work and life are remembered.

He was a pioneer, one of those who led the way into a new world; only his world was not beyond the mountains or the stars—it was the world of small things. In this world Louis Pasteur was an explorer and a hero. He entered this world through a microscope and fought his battles in a quiet laboratory. In his path he left the world a safer place in which to live, because of the discoveries he made and the inspiration he gave to scientists who followed.

Herschel Levit

SCIENCE STORY LIBRARY